No hair, no remorse

Reflections on working hard for little reward

W B Lower

Also from the same author:

Falling on Grim Times - Tales of Misadventure and Cleaning in the Midlands

From an Unknown Informant or Few

# Contents

Foreword by Mister Tea

Preface

Introduction

Chapter 1 - communication won't let you down, or will it?

Chapter 2 - bosses cannot be that idiotic can they?

Chapter 3 - the do it my way or feck off approach to management, does it work?

Chapter 4 - targets, targets, targets

Chapter 5 - Supervisors, no longer a worker, not quite management

Chapter 6 - favourites and the consequences of management having them

Chapter 7 - Tw@ts with stats

Chapter 8 - senior management / head office wtf are they thinking?

Chapter 9 - why bother training staff?

Chapter 10 - what goes around comes around, or simply reinventing the wheel?

Chapter 11 - manners cost nothing but recruiting new staff does

Chapter 12 - bullying, harassment and discrimination

Chapter 13 - teams sometimes hard to build yet easier to destroy

Chapter 14 - if it ain't broke don't fix it

Chapter 15 - should I join a trade union?

Chapter 16 - thinking ahead instead of reacting

Chapter 17 - feck being a staff number be a person first Chapter

18 - respect is a two way Street

Chapter 19 - mistakes and why learning from them makes far more sense than cover ups

Chapter 20 - cooperation and compromise are better than conflict

Chapter 21 - is it worth being self employed?

Chapter 22 - sometimes it's just one of them fecking days

Chapter 23 – the fine art of tossing it off

Chapter 24 - Robots, why have to deal with people?

Glossary - Words and phrases to be embraced by the cynical and avoided like the plague by management or the ambitious

# Foreword

Coming soon … saving it for the paperback

# Preface

So bosses often think they can get more out of their workers and then are surprised when more often than not they fail to do so. Yet bosses either deliberately or because they do not give a damn do not understand their workers. If they took the time to watch and listen to their staff then they could improve worker satisfaction as well as company performance. Workers can also learn when they have the opportunity to improve where they work, and when it is sometimes far more sensible to get a job somewhere else and leave at their earliest convenience.

Perhaps junior management and workers should consider that it is head office that could be the ones to blame for stress and low pay instead of finding fault with each other.

Undoubtedly, any managers reading these reflections would find them scathing in many ways.

How people look, and how people stare

Well I don't even think that I care

You rot your life away and what do they give?

Your just killing yourself to live!

The wise words of Geezer Butler in Killing Yourself to Live, by Black Sabbath released in 1973.

Having Ozzy sing that he likes to eat waccy cakes and might possibly swing both ways, that is simply genius...


'Technical School was a waste of time, making some robots for the factory line' Scarred for Life, Rose Tattoo, 1982


Colleague to me when I was younger: do you know if you are coming or going?

Me: I am not sure yet, I will let you know in about 30 years

For Elizabeth II – Thank you

To the Ukraimian nation - Slava Ukraini

Front cover photo – yours truly with my Nan circa early 1970s

# Introduction

In the last 30 years or so I have worked for at least 60 different firms and done around 100 jobs as well as working for myself sometimes. Some jobs have lasted only days while some lasted for a few years a time. All of these jobs have increased my levels of experience and added new skills every now and again. Many firms will have managers that have similar approaches while some have been more unique.

Managers and workers could both get more of what they want or need if they understood each other's needs better. Yet in most cases workers seem to understand their bosses better than their bosses understand them. Managers might not bother to learn or understand about the workers they manage as long as the required work is getting done. Sometimes managers make promises they have no intention of keeping, and others make threats. Workers though eventually learn the difference between the firms that keep their promises and those that do not, or the threats that are carried out and those, which are empty. Such knowledge can shape the decisions that workers make concerning where they work and wether they are prepared to stay there.

The following chapters will outline what I have personally learned during my working life, and the factors that have prevented that work making myself a fortune. Some things may be altered for comic affect, others to prevent the identities of people involved including myself being revealed.

Many thanks to Mister Tea for writing the foreword, a wise friend who strongly believes that there is never a bad time to drink a good cup of tea, especially on management's time. Personally I have aided and abetted his attempts to drink milky tea with 2 sugars many times. His a top bloke, I don't have managerial or supervisory permission to state so, but when did that ever stop me doing anything?

# Chapter 1 - communication won't let you down, or will it?

A major cause of problems or tensions between workers and managers is communication. To paraphrase 1980s pop group Spandau Ballet and their 1987 tune, communication won't let you down. Except more often than not it is how information is or is not communicated that can make or break a single workplace or an entire firm. How information is passed on and shared can vary from organisation to organisation as well as depending on whether the workers operate onsite or work remotely. In most places there will be routine tasks or work that always need doing and how management want things done is, or should be covered in training.
Sometimes there will be a need to complete ad hoc tasks that means workers and bosses would be well advised to discuss what needs to be done and the best ways to successfully achieve it.

Things can go wrong when there are changes whether planned and unplanned. Planned changes should not cause problems yet if managers fail to communicate the benefits of altering things workers can be uncertain of their futures. When things are planned communication should be more organised and effective than when changes are unplanned.

When planned changes are explained effectively by managers then these are more likely to be accepted by employees. Being accepted is not exactly the same as being liked, yet it generally means that there is less resistance to proposed alterations. Unplanned changes may pose more issues as managers are less likely to have time to prepare a response to altered circumstances.

Unplanned changes can demonstrate how capable management teams are to deal with events or circumstances they were not expecting. Some bosses are better than others and sometimes those who are better at keeping their people informed about things get a better response than those who fail to let workers know what is going on even if they make similar decisions or react in the same way. Communication during changing times can go a long way in reassuring workers concerned about what is happening, or possibly could take place.

In theory advances in technology improve both the quantity and quality of communication between bosses and workers. In practice, this is not always the case as bosses can send emails and texts to their staff without making sure these instructions or updates have been received as well as understood. Just because an email has been marked as read doesn't mean it has been read and certainly may not have been understood. If managers want to make sure that their messages or orders are going to be acted upon then they need to ask staff if they know what they are expected to do. Should the workers not understand any or all of what they have been informed about then the managers are best explaining things again. Bosses can be mistaken if they assume that silence from below equates to acceptance and full understanding of what needs to be done. It often means that instructions are so poorly worded that these do not make any sense at all, or that totally contradict current practices.

Now some bosses are actually willing to talk to their workers about orders or communications should they have any concerns or queries. This willingness to discuss things makes the relationship with workers better than if bosses are not willing to discuss or clarify any issues. Workers that do not believe they can freely discuss issues or talk to their bosses are less likely to be content in their position and more likely to consider finding gainful employment somewhere else. People that feel ignored may chose to either shout out, shut up or simply jump ship. Perhaps if the number of staff leaving has increased significantly it could be a sinking ship, which they are departing from.

Communication is also about listening as well as talking. Sometimes in work places bosses and workers are so concerned about getting their points across that they do not even attempt to appreciate or understand what the other is saying. In other words work relations are aided by bosses and employees having conversations with each other instead of slanging matches. Most of all they need to listen to one another. Listening enables those do it to learn things they would not find out simply by talking at the same time as others, if not talking over them.

Acronyms and jargon can also cause communication problems, particularly when not everybody uses it. If sending emails, letters or reports to others teams, or externally your company should then either cut out jargon or clarify what it means.

## Chapter 2 - bosses cannot be that idiotic can they?

Boss : Why didn't you answer all the phone calls?

Worker : Because there are six phones, 2 people with days off, 2 people rang in sick, and Jim is on his dinner.

Meanwhile a few years later...

Supervisor : I want you to take a picture of what is wrong at this part of the warehouse.

Me : Would that be using the phone that you made me put in a locker this morning at the start of the shift?

The short answer to that question is, yes they can be that idiotic and then some. Plus the further up the managerial ladder they are, the dafter their decisions can be. The further away from the shop floor bosses are, the further away from reality they might be,

Just about every organisation I have worked in, or for has had moments when questionable if not downright fecking stupid decisions have been reached at the top and expected to be followed by everyone that they apply to. Then there are countless other examples from other companies that managerial common sense is a very rare commodity indeed. People that work anywhere that has sensible bosses who make logical and relevant decisions should count themselves as being lucky.

Fortunately most of the time, if companies are operating to their usual routine then bosses and workers can stick to how things are normally done without too many problems. Lower management ranks and supervisors may even revert back to old ways of doing things if senior managers do not pay too much attemtion as how to things are done. It can be when something needs to be done differently that poor decisions are made. It is the workers that have to make sure their work is done in accordance with new decisions and are most likely to be blamed if the results are not what management expected or wanted. Workers that complain about decisions and changed work practices can be disliked or distrusted by managers even if worker feedback is a sound evaluation of why things are failing.

Bosses who feel there is no limit on their authority to make and enforce decisions can potentially make the worst choices by not consulting colleagues, workers or seeking experts from outside of the company. The failure to consult others that could have relevant or useful knowledge can mean that incorrect or unwise decisions are made. Taking into account all the relevant information should improve the chances of any boss reaching the best possible decision available to them. The higher the quality of the information available to managers the better chances of reaching a logical decision.

Managers who fail to consult workers or seek information from outside sources that understand the issues they need to make decisions on are risking things going wrong. Capable but stubborn managers can cause damage than less able ones that are prepared to compromise or at listen when reaching decisions. Those bosses that ask workers opinions about issues when considering changes or as part of the decision making process before going ahead and implementing what they wanted to do anything are worse than those that don't consult at all. Workers who are consulted and then completely ignored are more annoyed with the boss than those who were never asked at all. Personally once I know that a manager asks for feedback or opinions then disregards it , then I will not waste my time again. Bosses that continue to ignore their workers will eventually get nothing from them in terms of cooperation or information.

The bosses that are convinced that they are always right are arguably those most prone to make the idiotic decisions. When someone is confident that they are right about their decisions then tend to go full steam ahead with getting their decisions turned into reality. It is when poor decisions are put into practice at the shop floor level that the workers are left to make the unworkable work. That leaves workers with the dilemma of working harder to achieve less, or be looked down upon by management. Yet there is no logical reason to work harder for less progress than before. Rushing around , working harder and faster to make the unworkable work is nonsense. Workers that feel really alienated from the management may simply leave and go work somewhere else. Besides the harder people work the more that management take the extra effort for granted, and only very rarely will they express any thanks or appreciation for it.

# Chapter 3 - the do it my way or feck off approach to management, does it work?

Boss : Is everybody happy with working towards higher targets with no extra pay and the previous bonus cut in half?

All : We are absolutely delighted boss, can't wait to get started.

Two weeks later...

Boss : Where is everybody?

Secretary : Five finished last week, four are working their notice this week, warehouse on the next industrial estate pays more and the bonus is twice as much as ours.

Some bosses have a very high opinion of themselves and believe their workers should obey instructions and orders without question. For the purposes of this book I decided to dub this as the do it my way or feck off approach (or the I think I know it all but I know feck all way). Now those that adopt this approach to management may regard it is as sensible way of running the office, store or warehouse they are in charge of. These bosses are being optimistic at best and downright delusional at worst. Now personally I have had a strong urge to never do as I am told unless I really have to. It's definitely a case of muttering under my breath "yes boss, no boss, shove it where the sun never shines boss."

Perhaps the main reason for bosses using such a method to run their workforce is to reduce the number of complaints they receive from their charges. Bosses with the perspective that they do not want complaints or other general whinging from workers are blocking an avenue for employees to air their grievances or provide feedback. Not listening to employees when they are providing feedback or complaining can further their feelings of being cut off and alienated. This approach leaves the workers with no doubts as to whose in charge, while at the same time making them more likely to resent, or even resist such authority. A silent workforce should never be assumed to be a happy workforce, but it could certainly be a seething one. Workers may decide to eventually resist an autocratic boss, or they just leave. Once somebody has decided to leave they will tend to just turn up and do as little as possible, no amount of cajoling is going to make them work hard again.

Bosses that order workers around and expect no resistance should also expect no cooperation or enthusiasm from their staff. Workers that know the boss doesn't care what they think will not care about how well they perform their duties and will not be bothered to work hard. They turn up for shifts and only go through the motions and know they are getting paid for it. While bosses use this approach workers are not going to bust a gut, and those that did so under the last boss will stop doing so. This approach destroys the goodwill of workers, and that can be difficult to get back. Bosses that disregard the goodwill of their staff will lose it all together and that can drastically reduce what gets done.

While some people may feel intimidated by managers with such an approach more could be annoyed by it instead. Workers with more experience or self confidence may regard this managerial approach as providing enough motivation or excuse to leave the company and find another firm that will treat them better. After all if a boss cannot treat their workers with respect then they should not be surprised if those same workers decide to go to another company for employment. It is therefore an approach to management that can lead to an exodus of staff, which leaves bosses without enough staff to run the business effectively, at least until replacements have been hired and trained. Staff may stay while looking for other jobs, or because they cannot afford to leave their current job yet they will remain unhappy and underperforming members of the team unless their boss leaves, or adopts a friendlier approach. It is doubtful though that anybody deluded or big headed enough to adopt this approach in the first place is going to change their behaviour, after all as far as they are concerned they are right and everybody else is wrong. There is no point being the only person who is right when everybody has left.

Another way for workers to react to the do it my way or feck off approach to management is to complain about the bosses who adopt it. For example, they could complain to higher managers and state that they are not satisfied with how they are being treated. This could lead to the issue being looked into, depending on the company's structure and internal procedures. In companies that allow trade unions the complaints could by raised by shop stewards. Senior managers could consider replacing bosses that are upsetting too many of their staff, or even request that they change their approach.

In my experience it is very rare for anybody arrogant (and possibly deluded) enough to adopt this approach to management to change it. They would rather have no staff than back down at all, or even feck off somewhere else themselves, if their workers have forced higher management to intervene. After all backing down would be admitting that they had got something wrong, and they could never lower themselves to admit they had got anything wrong. Eventually this kind of manager will fail, and the longer it takes for them to do so, the more spectacular their fall from grace is. Yet before they fail these type of managers can do a great deal of damage if nobody above them in the managerial chain knows what is happening, or if superiors are not prepared to take action.

# Chapter 4 - targets, targets, targets

Team leader : Since we moved you to another team your replacement has done everything 5 times faster but accuracy has dropped from 95 to 15 %, can you give us any advice?

Me : Don't let your coffee go cold.

Team leader : You are not going to help the team?

Me : It is not my team since you moved me upstairs, it's no skin off my nose.

Team leader : It makes the team look bad. We used to meet the quality and quantity targets, yet now we process things quicker but with more errors.

Me : I warned you what would happen and why, but you ignored me, I am not telling you twice.

In recent decades it has become common practice to give both bosses and workers targets to measure how they are doing in terms of performance. Public and private sector organisations use targets to monitor how people are doing, and the achievement of such objectives can be a distraction or obsession that actually does more harm than good. Management can use the setting of targets to find a workable balance between quantity and quality. Unless a workforce is experienced and uses highly reliable equipment and procedures it is really difficult to get enough quantity at an acceptable level of quality. Bosses tend to stress quantity over quality especially when there is a heavy workload or a peak time in terms of orders. When the amount of work is lower then they may realise quality levels need to be improved.

Head offices in private companies and Secretary of States in the public sector can set targets that managers and workers nationwide have to achieve. These targets are left to managers to oversee whether these are realistic or not. Bosses are under pressure to make sure that all workers meet personal targets, and that is built into managerial objectives. The importance attached to targets is in some cases inane to the point of gross stupidity, and causes far more harm than good. Targets can be set so high that the only way that managers and workers could achieve these is to cut corners, or find means to fiddle the figures. Inaccurate data, or higher stats achieved by cutting quality can fool those in charge that the emphasis placed on meeting targets is working. Yet in reality inferior work is being performed, and may eventually have to be done again.

How targets are measured and whether or not these be altered when bosses and workers perform different tasks can cause debate. For instance, some tasks are more complex than others so should those performing harder work have lower targets than those doing the easier things?

So one member of staff may only complete ten tasks a day, compared to other colleagues that complete 100 a shift, yet these tasks are far simpler to perform. Some bosses may notice the difference in difficulty, while others may just assume that those who do 100 tasks a shift are better than those who complete 90 less, and think the faster workers are better. The fair thing to do would be to rotate who was doing the harder tasks, or weight 10 easy tasks as being equal to a single difficult task.

When trade unions are allowed to form their stewards can be critical of how targets are set and what the potential consequences for people that consistently fail to meet them are. Targets that are impossible, or virtually impossible to achieve are in reality of no use to bosses or workers. Excessively high targets stress people, sometimes to the point of being detrimental to their physical health and mental well being. Over the long term such targets cause far more damage than good. Perhaps the only purpose unreasonably high targets serve is to provide an excuse to get rid off the workers, who fail to reach them. Workers that have access to a trade union are well advised to consult their steward if their personal performance is failing targets and leaving them with the threat of being disciplined. In work places without trade unions workers may find it harder to keep their jobs if they regularly fail to meet their quotas.

If set to be achievable and realistic targets can serve useful purposes for both bosses and workers. Yet when objectives are drawn up that cannot be met even with Herculean efforts then these should be changed for realistic ones instead. High targets can be set due to the most senior managers having unrealistic expectations of what can be done by those people below them. They will notice the numbers achieved by the best performers instead of evaluating average numbers. Their argument would be that if some workers can meet or even exceed targets then all workers can at least achieve the quotas. They may even ignore the reasons why the highest performers have such high numbers compared to everybody else, such as being given easier tasks, having greater experience, or using better equipment. Sometimes targets may only be achieved due to staff doing overtime.

The aim of senior management is to increase the amount of work done, and in the private sector at least increase productivity and profit. However, unrealistic targets can often have the opposite impact and lower productivity and also revenue. Failed targets can be used as a reason for firing underperforming managers or workers if they do not decide to leave for pastures new without high stress levels and for fairer treatment. The thoughtless pursuit of targets often wastes time, effort and money. The faster people work especially with less experience and poor training the faster mistakes are made.

It would make far more sense to do things properly and keep errors to a minimum, instead of working much faster and getting more things wrong. Remember that the more members of staff that have to deal with a task to get it right, the more time and money is being wasted, better to do it right than do it fast. There is little point in doing 100 tasks per hour if 95 are wrong and things are either below standard, or have to be done again. Surely it would make more sense to do 50 an hour and only get 2 or 3 things wrong?

I have noted in various roles that new staff members can be keener about achieving targets than more experienced colleagues. Perhaps new workers want to impress the supervisors and the managers (at least until they pass probationary periods) while experienced team members may have got cynical about the targets.

# Chapter 5 - Supervisors, no longer a worker, not quite management

Supervisor : Why aren't you going for your break now?

Assistant 1 : It is too early to have our lunch now.

Assistant 2 : You are not the boss, you can't make us do anything.

Supervisor : Well in that case I will inform the manager that you ignored their instructions.

Aside from a few months in my mid 20s being a supervisor is something I have managed to avoid . I have always thought that the little extra bit of pay is simply not worth the extra stress. Some companies barely pay their supervisors anything extra at all, even managers may get a measly amount on top of the workers' pay rate, certainly not enough to justify the greater amount of stress they often have to endure. Be a manager for a few miserable pence over minimum wage? Are you having a laugh?

Mind you , I have known a fair number of colleagues that have regarded being promoted to a supervisor as an excuse to begin chucking their weight about. Well depending on their personalities some got away with it, and others got ignored. How much authority supervisors have is subject to variations from company to company. Supervisors in reality only have power delegated from the managers and there are limits in most cases about they can do.

A minority of companies in my experience hire their supervisors from outside their workforce. Most tend to promote from within as the new supervisors already know and understand the company and what needs to be done. It can save money on recruitment costs and there is a reduced or no settling in period. Individuals promoted from within have to consider how it alters their relationship with both workers and managers. They have to tell people what to do even though they might have considered themselves friends before promotion. Workers do not always find it easy to be told off by somebody who used to be equal with them until recently. More ambitious supervisors may not be bothered about losing closeness with workers and instead concentrate on closer ties to management. After all a stronger bond with managers in theory enhances their chances of further promotion. Sometimes promotion is gained on merit, other times on been the right person in the right place, most times it is arguably down to having good connections with the people that matter in terms of making appointments. Supervisors appointed on merit usually have a higher potential for further promotions.

Supervisors can play valuable roles in been the links between workers and managers. They can communicate to workers about any changes that management have brought in, as well as well passing back feedback from workers regarding what is working and what is not. Sometimes workers may tell supervisors their complaints or concerns when they would tell managers. That may be on condition that supervisors pass the information on without revealing who said what.

They could also provide information to management that is detrimental to workers but doing so would mean the workers would no longer trust them (if they had done previously). Supervisors that succeed are most likely to do so by doing all that management ask of them without alienating the workers at the same time. Anybody that can maintain that delicate balance most of the time is doing well. Getting the balance right could help them to get promoted in the future as well. Some managers promote supervisors due to their abilities, some are moved up the chain due to their loyalty, while others get promoted mainly because of how long they have been there.

There are some supervisors that only want to reach that far, and do not have ambitions to be promoted further. These are the ones that could be more likely to be closer to the workers than the managers. Less ambitious supervisors may also be less likely to tell management information that could detrimental to some colleagues. On the other hand individuals that regard being a supervisor as a stepping stome for further promotions are more willing to do management's bidding and regard themselves as part of the management team. Supervisors can find themselves in a difficult position when relations between staff and managers are poor, especially during strikes. What side they take during disputes could well decide the direction their career goes in, depending on how management react after the dispute is over.

# Chapter 6 - favourites and the consequences of management having them

About 20 years ago...

Team Leader : Well Bill the bad news is that the moderating meeting decided that your performance did not meet expectations this year and therefore you did not earn your bonus.

Me : Well that will teach me the virtues of being an ar*se licker like Thomas, Richard and Harriet.

Team Leader : There is no need to be so cynical. By the way, why have you stopped doing over time?

Me : Well apparently my work is sh*t, and I would like to see my wife and kids occasionally.

A few years later at a different office a team leader contrived to move her 3 least favourite staff...

Team Leader : As none of you would volunteer to go over to the Reviews section 3 names were pulled from a hat. I am sorry to see Glen, Bill and Lizzy go (the smug grin on her face amply demonstrated her insincerity).

Glen to me and Lizzy on the way to Reviews : Well that was 7 pieces of paper with Glen on, 7 with Bill on and the last 7 with Lizzy on!

It is very much part of human nature to have favourite things and indeed people. Everyone will have a favourite colour, football team, drink or person to work with etc. Yet in the context of workplaces having favourites can cause problems and even conflicts. Managers often have favourite workers, workers frequently have favourite supervisors and bosses.

Having a favourite or a few favourites may cause issues in a workforce depending on how subtle or overt bosses are about it. Letting a favourite go to break a couple of minutes early is mildly annoying, refusing to discipline them for any act that should be regarded as gross misconduct could cause major dissent in the ranks. A manager who is subtle with the favours they allow some staff will mostly avoid really annoying the rest of the team. Yet allowing a favourite to go on a fortnight cruise during the peak period when nobody is allowed extra time off just annoys the feck out of everybody else.

When a manager gets jokes from workers that they should change their name to that of a favourite, or put on a wig to look like them, then it is time to stop giving their favourite such obvious favours. Constant overt favours to a favourite are going to cause resentment and disharmony in any team. Such resentment and disharmony is completely avoidable by managers reducing the favours to certain people and treating everyone in the team equally. Alternatively managers could give out rewards on the basis of merit, for instance to the person with the most sales, or the worker that dealt with the most phone calls, or to the individual that provided the best piece of customer service.

Workers can also have favourite supervisors or managers and would prefer to work for them than anybody else. They may work harder or smarter for their favoured bosses compared to ones they do not particularly like. Managers who treated the workers in their team fairly and with respect are more likely to have a willing workforce than not. Some workers may even change jobs to continue working with their favourite managers.

Another way that managers can have favourites is by selecting certain workers to work in their sections or on their shifts. They do this to attempt to manage the best performing teams as some companies give bonuses to such teams. Getting all the best performers together should mean all targets are achieved and then some. Other teams may resent the creation of elite teams yet the highest level of management will be content that it means productivity and revenue increases. Managers may also have to find ways to prevent their best workers being headhunted by other managers. While teams may be more competitive it may do nothing to improve harmony between all teams within the company.

Sometimes in larger organisations there may be times when managers have to compete with each other to get favours for their favourites. They may have to do bargains and other staff miss out so that favourites can receive perks and rewards, which are not deserveed or other members of staff should have got instead. Managers' pets get rewards and sometimes the people that do all the work getting absolutely nothing. Personally I learned the hard way that working harder and going the extra mile is completely pointless when you are not a manager's favourite.

People will sometimes make deliberate attempts to become bosses' pets, these are ar*se lickers / brown nosers, and some of them seem to have no dignity at all. They will do anything to become favourites and stay that way. These people may put far more effort into being a managerial pet than they put into carrying out their jobs. Yet if they get enough perks out of their status as a favourite then they will believe that such efforts are worth making. Being overly nice to bosses may make all the difference between actually having to work for a living, or tossing it off and doing very little work evey single shift. Blatent ar*e licking can certainly get creeps with no shame rewards yet at the cost of losing the respect of colleagues.

When in the civil service I worked longer hours and overtime but got stitched up at more than one moderating meeting with my annual performance review downgraded to give an undeserving colleague a bonus. The lesson was learned not to put myself out any longer. Yet before I learned that lesson I missed out on seeing my kids as much as I should have, too dedicated to a job in, which the managers didn't appreciate me and gave rewards for those that did far less for the team. It made me even more of a cynical bast**d than I already was.

Don't repeat my mistake when not the manager's pet, put family and friends ahead of the job. There is no point in putting the job first because apart from over time there is very little to gain from doing so.

# Chapter 7 - Tw@ts with stats

Planner : If we put two people to each desk then we can double the output of the office. It might make the crazy amount of rent paid for the office worth it.

Project Manager : Yes but that output will be of a low quality because you won't give us enough time to train the new recruits properly.

Sometimes business decisions are based solely on nameless people at headquarters looking at data, or tw@ts with stats as I like to say. Such decisions can completely ignore any input from either managers or workers. No wonder some decisions seem so unrealistic and the targets people are set are really hard to reach. If the people in charge of the stats have actually worked on the shop floor there is the tiny glimmer that sensible decisions are made. It is more likely that these people with stats have never done the job themselves and have no ideas about the difficulties and issues that could hamper targets been met.

These people that prefer looking at stats on their laptops whether intentionally or inadvertently can make life miserable for all those that have to achieve the targets they set sometimes hundreds of miles away from the shop floor. Perhaps the laptops are surgically attached to some part of their bodies as they never seem to let them go. Perhaps laptops are attached to their wrists to prevent theft as well as stopping the users having a life outside of their job. I have visions of them bursting into tears if the laptops break or the system crashes.

Those data collectors or analysts can and do make peoples lives miserable by increasing pressure on them. Data and stats can be used to work out those who are performing best and those who might improve with more training and encouragement.  However, data can be used as a stick to get people to work harder to meet performance targets, and as a reason to discipline or fire staff. Stats can also be used to reward top performers, or those that are favoured by senior managers or the data management team.

Stats should be used to inform senior managers about those things that their organisation is doing and those things that are going wrong or could be improved. Management can manipulate stats or ask the data experts to manipulate stats to make the situation within their organisation appear better or worse than it actually is for their own purposes. Governments can be even worse than private companies for attempting to manipulate stats for their own means, though the new data may be questioned.

Stats can be used to get people promoted, rewarded or conversely fired if that is what suits the powers at be best. Those that collect and analyse data and turn into stats that the most senior managers can use are generally doing what they are told. Rarely they might not like the purposes stats are used for and turn whistleblowers. Most of the time though they will put up or move elsewhere, like most of the rest of us. Anybody who has ever studied politics or history even for a short time should realise that stats can be used for all kinds of purposes and the most sinister of reasons.

Stats can be altered to actually present a false image of what happened, or what is happening. Just slight variations in how data is collected and analysed can have a profound impact on what the stats show. So stats can be changed to make a failure seem a success, or even to portray something that succeeded as being a failure. It pays to have a degree of caution when faced with particularly if what it is being used to demonstrate seems far too good to be true.

# Chapter 8 - senior management / head office wtf are they thinking?

Visiting manager from head office : why is everybody complaining about the new layout for this store?

Ofiice manager : Well you had two different groups plan the changes, the first group measured everything in feet and inches, while the second group measured everything in metres and centimetres. It might not have been a problem if each group had specified, which system they had used instead of just jotting down numbers on the plans. Some teams have too much space, and others don't have enough.

Workers, supervisors and junior managers might regularly ask what the hell that the most senior management team or their head office are thinking about when certain decisions are made and why these should possibly be reconsidered.

The most senior managers depending on the size of their organisation can be a long way both physically and metaphorically from the shop floor so can make poor decisions through lack of communication or knowledge. Top bosses need to have information concerning what is happening at all levels below them to have a clear picture of reality. That is often not the case as middle and high levels of management do not always pass on what low level bosses, supervisors and workers are telling them. Perhaps they don't want to be bearers of bad news or afraid of making the senior management team angry. Some poor decisions can be put down to a lack of relevant information.

To be blunt some poor decisions are due almost entirely to the people at the top being more obtuse than two short planks nailed together. Daft ambitious people with a ruthless personality and good connections will often get further than more sensible people that couldn't be bothered with the extra stress that continuous promotions could give them. Thick people in high places either not been told what is going on, or ignoring what they are told is usually a recipe for things going pear shaped. And then some...

Those employed in some capacity by the civil service and government departments can also be affected by government decisions, or sometimes lack of them. Civil servants right from the permanent secretary all the way down to the lowest ranking pen pusher are supposed to be politically neutral. Yet a dim and ideologically minded Secretary of State no doubt taking the orders from a potentially even dimmer Prime Minister can make all sorts of silly decisions (i e the mini budget that cost Liz Truss her post as PM). About once a decade some plonker in Downing Street will decide there are too many civil servants and make thousands redundant. Then within a couple of years more need recruiting as there is nobody to do essential paperwork.

Those that work in the civil service may feel a strong sense of deja vu when ministers change policies. After all, policies or strategies previously tried and abandoned often come back a few years later and usually with a different name. A new name, same old cr*p. There is the option the ambitious staff take of not saying anything and letting senior management eventually learn that things are not working. Cynical individuals like myself call a turd a turd and will say I told you so when it goes wrong. Such a cynical approach usually means there is very little hope of ever getting promoted.

Not that promotion can be worth the stress that it all too often brings, pressures worsened when senior management or head offices have little clue about what is going on and want everybody who works for them to make the impossible actually happen. Should the impossible or the improbable be achieved then they will expect such a feat to be emulated on a regular basis. Most people cannot perform miracles yet some like to try to do so, and others will claim to have done so in order to advance up the management ladder.

# Chapter 9 - why bother training staff?

Manager : Why can't you do as much work as the experienced staff?

New starter : Because I was only given 5 minutes to see how the job is done, and nobody showed us what to do when anything goes wrong.

Some bosses do not see the point of training their staff yet still expect them to perform their jobs effectively. While some jobs are harder to do, and learn how to do than others, there are good reasons why full and appropriate training is given to staff.

Managers need to consider how much training new recruits and the workers already there require. Some jobs are considerably more complex, some need to use complex equipment. Companies will often attempt to keep the training of new recruits to a minimum by hiring staff that have experience in the same or similar roles. If they are unable to hire experienced workers then they should provide extra training depending on what the new staff understand about their jobs. Basic training should cover the use of all gear and equipment they would be expected to use, appropriate health and safety issues as well as fire regulations. In other words that workers are competent in their jobs and can remain safe in emergency situations. Bosses may change the level of training provided depending on whether new recruits are meant to be temporary or permanent members of staff. They would see little point in providing full training for people leaving within a month or two.

Some training is mandatory and employers are legally obligated to provide it to all staff. There can be legal consequences if such training is not provided, particularly if there are accidents that result from worker being untrained. Some companies may try to get around this by offering minimal amounts of training. If workers are concerned that training is inadequate and that puts them at risk they should contact health and safety teams, or trade Union reps if available.

Managers should consider offering extra training to staff that might benefit their performance levels. If bosses are concerned that workers are not doing as well as they could be then further training may help to raise their productivity. Perhaps extra training is needed as the original training was not wide ranging enough or did not cover the right topics.

Training should be given whenever new equipment, procedures or IT systems are introduced to make sure staff can work in new ways. Larger companies and organisations should give serious consideration to running pilot schemes to evaluate how the new system or equipment works, whether it is better or worse than what it is intended to replace. In extreme cases if the pilot schemes indicate that the new ways will not work then the changes should be abandoned. However most places do not have senior management teams that are that proactive, or have lower and middle ranking managers that do not tell them that the new ways are not going to work. So when senior managers are not warned that the changes are not going to work then they will proceed full steam ahead. Then again, sometimes they are warned and still carry on regardless. Usually when that happens it is the workers and lower levels of management are left to sort out the mess, with little or no extra training.

Some training has to be provided because it is mandatory to do so, for instance health and safety, equal opportunities and fire regulations. Companies and organisations, which do not provide such training at all can be fined or prosecuted. Managers, supervisors and workers who purposely avoid such training can also face legal consequences for doing so. While mandatory training can seem dull especially when it has to be done every year but it needs to be done, and all that staff can do it should take all the information on board as it can be highly important to know.

# Chapter 10 - what goes around comes around, or simply reinventing the wheel?

During a weekly staff meeting...

Office manager : well head office have decided that thngs need changing around. Again. The old hands sre going to groan when I tell you what they are bringing back. No doubt they will change their minds again in a few months.

Managers should always be thinking about ways they can make things better. Sometimes they suggest changes because they were bored and want to alter things just to have things to do. Some alterations can be original and have never been used before. Others have been tried before even if the current bosses were not responsible for using those things in the past.

When changes are introduced some managers will argue that the future is here early and here to stay. Yet others will state that the changes will only stay in place if these are more effective than what went on before. Changes need to be given time to work, with senior management being given feedback that accurately reflects the failures or successes of all updated work procedures or new systems. It is a difficult balance between not giving changes enough time to work, or giving them too much time when if senior management was given accurate feedback it would show the changes were not fit for purpose. Sometimes if new systems or procedures are deemed to be failures then the powers at be will decide to revert back to what was previously in use. While that has the advantage that staff are familiar with it , the old way of doing things may no longer be the most efficient way to get the job done. Yet an old system that still works is better than no system at all, until a better solution can be put in place.

Occasionally old practices and procedures are brought back by members of senior management teams who had not been there when these had been dropped. Therefore these managers are probably not aware of why the old ways of doing things had been abandoned, and will only focus on the perceived advantages of bringing these back. Staff that remember the old ways may have mixed opinions as to whether or not their revival is good or bad.

New managers may not realise that they are reviving an old system because they believe that they have developed a completely new one, and even give it a new name or title. Lower managers and workers that have been in the organisation for a longer period will almost certainly note that the newly announced procedures or system are very similar if not exactly the same as an earlier one. Definitely a case of what goes around comes around.

Now bringing in new procedures or systems on a regular basis , abandoning them, then reviving them a few years later can be a waste of time, money and other resources. Perhaps it would make sense to adopt one system and keep it for as long as possible before replacing it. That would reduce the need to chop and change so much.

By reverting back to something that has been used before the members of staff that used the system should only need refresher training or none at all. Staff that have used a system before may regard it as a sensible step back to something that actually does what it is supposed to, or simply swapping a new system that doesn't work for an older one that doesn't do the job either. Once again if senior management are sensible they should consult staff to find out their views on the advantages and disadvantages of procedures and systems being considered.

Lower levels of management, supervisors and workers can have preferred procedures and systems, that may vary depending on their specific roles, when they joined the company and if these make their tasks easier to complete. Senior managers would almost certainly evaluate performance and productivity stats too when deciding whether to change systems or not.

# Chapter 11 - manners cost nothing but recruiting new staff does

Received a phone call about 25 years ago...

Superior : Bill don't come to work on Monday as your fecking fired.

The following day he called back.

Supervisor : Do you want your fecking job back?

Me – Feck off.

(I know that decision paid off because a couple of jobs later I met my wife).

Now some managers and supervisors have the impression that how they treat their staff has little baring on how well they work, or how long they are prepared to stay in their jobs. Those people are incorrect in their assumptions, workers that are unhappy with how they are treated by their superiors are less likely to perform their roles effectively, and more likely to seek employment opportunities elsewhere. Managers that could not even be bothered to be civil with their workers are not doing the right thing, they are always going to end with a team that performance drops, and loses it's members at a faster rate than other parts of the company. Being rude, aggressive, or even just ignorant towards workers are sure ways to get people to leave. All rude managers are making staff turnover worse than it has to be, as the more people leave the greater the money that needs to be spent on recruiting and training replacements.

Unnecessary staff turnover can be averted by managers and supervisors showing good manners to their workers. Asking workers to do their tasks politely is far better than barking orders at them. People resent being shouted at, and are far more likely to willing perform tasks when they have been asked nicely. Also when tasks are completed workers will appreciate a thank you. A sensible boss will always thank their workers at the end of the shift for working hard. An appreciated worker is one that is more likely to be willing to help their bosses and work hard. A bullied or ignored worker on the other hand is only likely to do the bare minimum. Bosses that ignore human nature and expect hard work from people they treat like a pile of cr*p are going to be disappointed.

Rude managers can upset their staff, and that means people will leave if behaviour doesn't change. Some workers may confront or stand up to abusive or rude bosses, arguably many others either put up with it, or they leave. Some companies have ways, in which staff can make complaints about management, more probably don't. Managers can limit the damage by being apologetic to the people they have upset. Some bosses though are not prepared to say sorry, and they have a greater risk of staff leaving the company.

Having orders barked at them is not the best way to motivate staff into doing tasks, yet it undoubtedly convinces some of them to leave. It often takes away their good will to work for the company in general, and the rude bosses in particular. Don't ask people to do anything nicely, or even in a civil manner, don't expect them to do anything over the bare minimum in their job description. The good will of workers is something that the tw@ts with stats cannot quantity but it can certainly make a difference to productivity as well as performance. Managers are better advised to preserve or create good will as opposed to destroying it. Going hand in hand with good will is being bothered to do the work at all. An entire workforce simply going through the motions is a recipe for nose diving productivity as well as a sharp decline in the quality of the work actually completed.

Supervisors and managers that have better manners and are polite to their workers are more likely to get more work out of them in both the short and long term. A please, a thank you and thanks for your hard work today are words or phrases that make workers more willing to do their jobs, and to do them well. Making workers feel welcome and appreciated goes a long way to building a team spirit, yet that spirit can be quickly banished by a rude manager.

Rude managers who believe that their poor attitude and bad manners have no costs for their respective companies are wrong. Whilst it might be difficult to quantify lost performance and productivity it would be relatively simple to work out increased recruitment costs. Should managers continue in the appalling attitude to staff then their particular office, store or branch may continue to have higher recruitment costs due to their higher staff turnover rate.

Sometimes it can be workers instead of managers or supervisors who are rude. Staff being rude may may have internal as well as external consequences. Within companies rude workers may be disliked by colleagues, supervisors and managers. Rudeness may lead to arguments, complaints besides giving those people with poor or no manners a bad reputation. If people are only rude to colleagues and not their superiors then they get away with it. No being rude to external customers or contacts could lead to these outside bodies complaining to the worker's company and asking that they be disciplined or even fired. Generally management will frown upon staff who are rude to customers and will fire people for gross misconduct if they consider that the company's reputation could be harmed.

Just remember that good manners are free, that having to apologise for being rude is best if never needed. Being polite may not always be the easy option if faced with obnoxious colleagues or exceedingly rude customers, yet being so can prevent your personal reputation being damaged.

# Chapter 12 - bullying, harassment and discrimination

Power in the Darkness

Stand up and fight for your rights

Talking about freedom to live your life as you want

(Power in the Darkness, Tom Robinson Band, 1978).

A dozen years ago, a customer hangs up on my African born colleague, I answer her next call…

Caller : Thank goodness I got through to somebody I can understand.

Me : How can I help today?

Caller : I want to know how my claim is progressing, your colleague doesn't seem to know how to do the job, who trained her?

Me : She was trained by our best trainers.

Caller : Where was she born?

Me : Salisbury I believe, but that is not relevant to your claim.

After the call…

Me : Well she was a lovely woman I would never want to meet.

Colleague : How did you know Harare was called Salisbury?

Me : Because I am not as ignorant as that caller.

Colleague : Why didn't you tell her that you trained me?

Me : Well I would have had to say that you do our job better than I do it.

Now this chapter is more serious than most of the other chapters of this book. That is because bullying, harassment and discrimination are definitely not matters to be laughed at. These behaviours can be very upsetting for those individuals on the receiving end, and organisations should have ways to tackle such behaviour within. People that suffer from being picked on can be depressed and it can cause mental harm over the short and long term.

Personally I would say I have experienced bullying, and have sometimes felt harrassed but have been fortunate not to go through being discriminated against. Yet I have witnessesed people in some if not all the places I have worked in suffer from all three. Now some people are more sensitive than others, before politically correct times, it was referred to as having a thicker skin. Noboby should have to put up with being abused at work, and needs to find out who they have to seek help from.

People should seek help and clarify their legal position, and seek redress under civil and employment laws if they have a strong against those who abused them. People who work in places that allow trade unions have the option of seeking advise from their union rep. These days most larger companies will have Human Resources that have the capacity to look into claims of any discriminatory behaviour aimed towards individuals.

People should always treat each other with respect and avoid being offensive to others. We do not all find the same things offensive, what one person regards as banter, others may believe is rude or plain discriminatory. If in doubt about the difference, people should refrain from making comments or gestures.

In theory the amount of discrimination experienced in workplaces should have declined with the anti discrimination training that companies have to provide.

# Chapter 13 - teams sometimes hard to build yet easier to destroy

Companies and workplaces that manage to build teams out of managers, supervisors and workers are arguably more likely to succeed compared to those with fractured or none existent teams. When teams have been built there is greater harmony between all members and all of them are prepared to put more effort into completing their tasks and helping each other to drive the team forward. Teamwork can achieve more than all it's members working in isolation and not cooperating with each other.

Many companies and organisations still have team building events and exercises in order to create or improve team spirit within their teams. Some will even hold such events on a regular basis to maintain team spirit, or renew it if the membership has changed markedly. The make up of most teams will change over time as people leave for other jobs, retire, move area, or stop working for other reasons. New members that are welcomed into the team are likely to find their feet sooner. Team spirit needs to be nurtured if any company achieves it, because once it is disrupted it can take a long time to be restored.

Any of the factors, issues or problems examined in the other chapters can have an impact on teams either alone or in combination with any of the others. Most of the time the breaking or disruption of teams is not deliberate, because doing so rarely benefits anybody. Teams can be harmed by any of their members, and sometimes by outside parties. Any manager, supervisor or worker can potentially be the one that starts the ball rolling in terns of damaging good will and cooperation within a team, either inadvertently or by design. All may not be lost if enough of the team members are willing to compromise and solve the grievances of those that are not happy.

Management decisions, especially those made at head office can have a detrimental impact on teams. Conversely, inane decisions forced on teams from above can bind teams tighter together providing these are not so bad that members leave in droves. Yet silly changes can ruin team spirit as all the members despair at the insanity of the situation.

Managers that do not listen to staff, or that enforce changes without consulting their workers risk harming team spirit. Just thinking about what they are doing, and how they are doing it could reduce the damage. That is assuming that managers would prefer not to damage teams.

Managers that go head long into introducing new procedures and systems without regard to the damage those changes cause to teams might want to break up teams. A tight knit team could put up more resistance to changes than a disunited or fractured one. Teams may have valid reasons not to approve of proposed changes, or managers could do a better job of arguing in favour of what they are aiming to achieve and why. Some managers want to changes when they take over to ones that are more in line with their image. Others on the other hand other managers prefer to leave teams alone if performance and productivity targets are being consistently met. Managers should consider whether the projected benefits of changes will still be achievable if teams are damaged by the introduction of those changes.

There are times when management will do it's best to make sure that teams are broken up to remake the company or organisation. That is most likely to happen when the management or owners have taken it over. New managers or owners make have liked the brand, products, or services a great deal yet they do not wish to keep the managers and some of the workers that made the company what it was when it was taken over. The obvious problem with such an approach is that it smashes what the company was about, possibly making it unappealing to customers and the surviving staff members. Recreating something completely has the real risk of turning a successful company into a failed one.

# Chapter 14 - if it ain't broke don't fix it

I can just hear my English teacher screaming at me not to use a double negative at this point. But never one for doing as I am supposed to do. Just because it is an old phrase doesn't mean it is any less useful than when it was first used (if you are that interested then do an internet search). People no matter what their position in a company can think about changing things, perhaps if there is a lull in their normal work tasks. Yet if current practices, systems and technology is still what is required of them then there may be no need to change things just for changes sake. For management the urge to change things should sometimes be resisted. Reviewing what currently works well and considering whether changes will make things better is always worth doing. Some can resist the instinct to tinker with things while others cannot

When whatever is in place keeps workers and supervisors working well enough to meet productivity targets as well as motivated enough to come in for every shift then why alter it. Senior management and tw@ts with stats though can come along and alter things because they believe that performance could be better , and don't bother to evaluate data that would demonstrate that the present system is the best one to have in place.

Sometimes systems that don't need fixing could do with being maintained or tweaked to keep them working at their best. Buying new equipment for the sake of it may only waste money and not always improve productivity, yet there may come a time when things have to be replaced due to fatigue or being obsolete. Replacing equipment to keep a tried and trusted system fully operational makes more sense than ripping it up and introducing a new system with no guarantee that it will work at all.

The times that it is most likely that a system is replaced when it is still performing effectively is when there is a change in senior management, or when a company has been taken over. New managers or owners often come in with new ideas and decide that they know what is best. Yet the new ways may not be the best way forward and could be detrimental to productivity as well as staff morale. Change for the sake of it, or to bring something new to a company without knowing enough about what works best can often do unnecessary damage, which could have easily been avoided.

# Chapter 15 - should I join a trade union?

Train conductor circa 1978: "We will shortly be arriving at Birmingham Moor Street. If you look to your left there is Longbridge where they make cr*p cars, except today is Saturday so they went on strike to watch Blues at home and the Villa away."

Apart from 4 years in the National Union of Students as a university student, I have spent only a few months as a union member. The NUS put me off unions because they were more talk than helping their members. With hindsight I would certainly consider joining a union in any workplaces that allow staff to do so. I strongly urge anybody reading this book to join unions for a variety of reasons.

British trade unions used to have more power than they do now (though that could change), they even brought down governments in the 1970s. The Thatcher government changed that by smashing the Miners Strike in 1985 and restrictive employment laws, many places have opted to stop unions from operating on their premises. Compare that to the 1970s when many workers worked in closed shops and had to join a union whether or not they wanted to.

Trade unions mainly exist to serve the interests of their members , though from time to time they have interfered in politics. Most but not all unions are linked to, and fund the Labour Party, individual members do not have to get involved unless they chose to. Growing up in the 1970s I vaguely remember workers such as those working for British Leyland making up flimsy excuses to strike on a Saturday so they could go to football matches and then working on the Sunday so they didn't lose any pay. Now though strikes have to be voted for by members for valid reasons or the unions can have their funds seized. Irresponsible strikes in the past make it harder for unions now, and companies that do not let unions at their sites can get away with more in terms of ignoring workers rights.

Since the UK left the EU, workers should join unions at any opportunity as Tory governments will use Brexit as an excuse to restrict worker's rights. It is unclear how much EU legislation will be repealed but once worker's protection has been reduced it might not be restored. A Labour government may not view restoring employment rights as a main priority when it gets into office.

Being a union member allows workers to take in a union rep if they have any discipline meetings, which can improve their chances of not being fired, or treated unfairly. Unions can arrange legal advise to their members as well, and represent them at industrial tribunals. All members have to do is pay a regular subscription to maintain their membership status.

The more people that are union members in any given workplace the more chance the union has of being able to safeguard members' rights as well as improving terms and conditions for all. The presence of a union may also mean that management may have to consider consulting their staff more frequently and also think about compromising to keep things ticking along. Some management teams are more prepared to deal with and talk to unions than others are, and are therefore more likely to avoid disputes.

# Chapter 16 - thinking ahead instead of reacting

At some point every single person is either thinking of the past, or living in the now. Sometimes though it is worth thinking ahead instead of reaching to changes in life in general or at work in particular. For example, senior management should contemplate what to do if the equipment or IT systems currently used are nearing the end of their usability and when and what by these will be replaced with. Evaluating what needs updating should allow management to plan when replacements are made by, whether these can be done internally or by outside contractors, plus whether or not staff will need any additional training. The costs and benefits of updating equipment and systems should also be considered well in advance. It is also sensible for larger companies and organisations to trial new things to evaluate their effectiveness before introducing them across the board. Such trials should highlight if changes will work, which ones will work with adjustments, and those that will not work meaning they need to be scrapped.

All companies and organisations should plan ahead when it comes down to all aspects of safety. It is no good thinking seriously about safety after staff have been injured or worse, or if work premises have been severely damaged if not destroyed. If accidents or incidents have led to major injuries or even deaths then these are investigated meaning that management, staff members and companies can be held accountable . While as a whole the majority of organisations stick to the letter of various safety legislation and regulations they might not always keep within the spirit of it. At busy times bosses may turn a blind eye to safety procedures being fully enforced to speed up work. Sometimes workers will cut corners to meet their targets risking their lives literally to please managers or the tw@ts with stats. I recommend nobody ever risks their neck to meet targets, ignoring safety procedures and not using the safety gear provided means workers are not insured and their bosses may not be liable should fatal accidents happen. I have been in a factory when a worker died as a result of not using safety gear, his family got nothing, the bosses lost a good worker and everything was closed while the incident was investigated. Personal safety should always take priority over work.

Managers should also think about staffing levels, for instance consider hiring temporary workers to cover busier periods, and whether to offer some of them permnment roles if others leave. If hiring extra staff it needs to be decided whether to start them all at the same time, or start fewer recruits more often to allow smaller training groups. Management should make sure there are enough experienced workers around to advise and help new starters. Time should be allowed for people to learn how to do the job properly before expecting them to match the targets that their team mates achieve. All too often though new staff tend to be thrown in the deep end and expected to achieve high numbers with accuracy during their first week or so.

More thinking ahead would take place if senior management spent more time on the shop floor and could witness how different teams or departments worked with each other. Then they could observe and ask about the issues that go well and any problems that potentially harm productivity or quality. Sometimes the people working on the shop floor will be able to provide better evaluations of what works and what doesn't than any accountant or engineer.

# Chapter 17 - feck being a staff number be a person first

I am not number, I am a free man, and my life is my own now

(The Prisoner, Iron Maiden from The Number of the Beast, 1982).

Far too many people would describe themselves by what they do for a living instead of who they are. I have met people that should have called themselves by their employee or staff numbers instead of their names. Whatever their position within the company they work in these highly dedicated people believe that they are indispensable and that everything would fall apart if they leave. Guess what?

In the majority of cases when people leave companies these carry on regardless , whether or not productivity changes is a moot point, companies continue to function. Dedicated managers and staff that spend every spare hour at work instead of being at home or elsewhere relaxing should consider that family and friends are more important than working to the point of making yourself ill.

Some people take work very seriously, others still care about their present roles, and there others that stopped giving a cr*p ages ago. Managers are more likely to get better performance out of those that are dedicated to their jobs to the point of forgetting about or neglecting the rest of their lives. For their own sanity and health people should try to avoid being so dedicated that they let life outside of work pass them by. Staff when possible need to avoid stress and working to the point of mental or physical exhaustion. People may take physical breaks from their roles yet they don't always realise the mental health problems work can cause them. Remember most job vacancies can be filled relatively quickly but people are unique individuals that can never be replaced once they have gone. Don't let work and related stress ruin your health or even worse.

So don't stress out, don't do more than is needed, and go home, put the kettle on and relax. Working to the point of being exhausted, or being stressed to the point of making yourself ill is not worth it. Especially when hard work is taken for granted and never thanked for. It can be even worse when management have their favourites who get all the rewards and special treatment, while the people who do the real graft receive nothing at all. If that sounds familiar then stop going the extra mile day in and day out, work to rule and do what tasks you are paid for.

# Chapter 18 - respect is a two way street

Perhaps in an ideal world it would be good if everyone liked each other. However nobody lives in an ideal world, and in it's absence the best we can hope for is mutual respect. At all times people should be respectful towards each other, if you are polite to others, they should return that politeness. In terms of work there is respect of a different kind, respect for the professional skills and attributes of others. This is the type of respect discussed in this chapter.

Some managers believe that they will get more out of their staff if they are liked, while others think that being feared is the key to success. They are wrong, being respected is more likely to have staff work for their managers.

Managers that treat their staff with respect are more likely to be well received than rude or abusive ones. When asked politely to do something people are more willing to complete the work than if they have been ordered tersely to do the same task. If asked nicely by a new manager or supervisor workers will begin with respecting them.

In response to the respect given from management, workers can also give respect in return. Polite even friendly behaviour towards management and supervisors helps to build a cooperative team. When workers have respect for management they will be more willing to do things and will demonstrate goodwill. As mentioned in earlier chapters, goodwill is a priceless commodity for any company or organisation to have, and respect especially when it is mutually shared throughout will improve levels of goodwill.

Companies that can help maintain mutual respect throughout their premises and their various teams are doing well. Those people that respect their colleagues, staff and bosses while getting it back from others are all helping their companies to keep on going.

# Chapter 19 - mistakes and why learning from them makes far more sense than cover ups

Yours truly gets into work and really needs to go to the toilet…

Colleague (PT as mentioned in Falling on Grim Times) : Hi Bill, what are you doing in here?

Me : Going redder than a lobster, it's the first time I have gone into the Ladies since a drunken weekend in Dublin 30 years ago.

Colleague: please concentrate next time you have to use the toilet!

Meanwhile, a few years previously...

Project Manager : Well last week when I told you to do all cases without the proper identity checks because head office ordered it, and your objections were added to mine. This morning they got back to me and stated that productivity went up 5000 % yet the the error rate went up 80000 % . So now folks we will have to spend the next month putting everything right that was done wrong last week.

There has not been a human being born that has never made a mistake, error of judgement, or got something wrong. As the old saying went to err is human. Perhaps the most common actions to making mistakes is to cover up, deny all knowledge, or own up and then attempt to learn from whatever went wrong. A mistake might be something minor such as serving someone a coffee instead of a tea (Mister Tea would disagree with me on that point and insist that whoever made such an error received a good talking to) or something catastrophic such as a general placing his army in the wrong position and thousands of troops being killed or captured as a result. When most of us make mistakes we make a quick decision on what to do next. Those snap decisions can either nullify the initial mistakes or make them worse. Such decisions can often be based on what causes the least serious consequences for the individuals that made the errors instead of what causes the least amount of damage over all.

There are numerous reasons for mistakes being made, and most of these could be avoided if precautionary measures are taken. Errors can result when staff have no or inadequate training, the relevant information is not available or viewed, or when people misjudge the situation they face. Perhaps the biggest cause of errors is when people are not concentrating on the task or process at hand, may be they are distracted and that leads to getting even the most common or simple tasks wrong. People can also be prone to misunderstanding instructions and procedures, especially newly introduced ones.

Small mistakes are easier to cover up and conceal than errors on a large scale yet if the reasons these are made regularly than they will happen time after time. Sometimes people will not realise they are making mistakes at all, and in a work context somebody needs to tell them what is been done wrong and how it is done correctly. When staff have been provided with full training there should be a reduced scope for mistakes. If training has been partial then workers may not have been nformed of the most effective ways of performing their tasks. Whenever procedures or equipment are altered there should be training given to all staff impacted by the changes to minimise errors and waste. Sometimes refresher training should be considered, particularly if some workers are making more errors than their colleagues.

There are times when mistakes are made as a result of people not caring about what they are doing. When staff or managers have lost the will to carry out their tasks then they will not be bothered if they work properly and do things right. Mistakes will only stop if these people start to care again, or if they go to work somewhere else instead. Management should attempt to make workers interested in their work to regain productivity and good performance to former levels with a lot less errors.

Companies that tend to focus on quantity over quality could find that more mistakes are made (provided that they are collecting data of course). The management of such companies may believe that increased productivity is more important than preventing loses from mistakes and breakages. More often than not reactive management teams cannot make their minds up about whether quantity is always a priority over quality, and the occasional panic that too many mistakes have been made. Minor mistakes on a small scale would probably not be too detrimental overall yet the greater the volume of errors the higher the risks of causing greater losses to the companies concerned.

# Chapter 20 - cooperation and compromise are better than conflict

Big Security Guard : you are so short, thin and old you could not sort out a violent customer

Short Security Guard : I don't have to son, I only have to chat to them and calm everything down. Charge me and I show you what I would do if one attacked me.

So the big guard charges at the short guard who flings him over his shoulder…

Big Security Guard: how did you do that?

Short Security Guard : I have black belts in several martial arts as well as being an unarmed combat instructor in the Commandos for 15 years. Yet knowing how to talk and listen to people then compromising with them goes further than hitting anybody ever did.

There is nothing better than getting your own way all the time, in theory at least. The more people in a company or organisation the harder it is for anybody to get anything they want even for the shortest amount of time. Perhaps only the chair people and the presidents of companies have any prospect of getting what they want. As previous chapters discuss there are limits to power, and if staff are unhappy about senior management being too overbearing then they will leave.

Companies and organisations whatever their management might believe function better when those within it cooperate and compromise with each other. It means that all team members are gaining something from been part of the team, and are also contributing towards it being a success.

Calming down tense situations will help to limit and even stop conflict. The key is to stop people shouting at each other. When arguments are getting too heated then voices are raised to the point that the main protagonists are shouting. When it gets to that point it proves that everyone has stopped listening. This is when someone or a few people have to step in and get those arguing to slowly and quietly put forward their perspective in the dispute. When all sides of the argument have been heard it should become clearer if there are any realistic chances of compromise.

It might result in reverting back to what a primary school teacher would have done. See if people are prepared to shake hands after the dispute has ended, consider having them work apart at least until tensions have eased, or have to agree to disagree.

# Chapter 21 - is it worth being self employed?

A few years ago…

My wife : How much have you earned this week?

Me : About £95 give or take.

My wife : How many hours have you worked to get that?

Me : 75 I think .

Shortly after that I went back to working for agencies just to pay more of the bills.

Some people prefer to be self employed than working for companies as an employee. Being your own boss means that you decide when and where you work. Sometimes you may have plenty of work and work 80 hours a week to do it in. Other times there may be little work available and you might have to use up savings or get shifts as an employee just to get by.

The amount that can be earned from self employment can vary greatly depending on what field people decide to work in. The more specialist or skilled it is, the greater the potential earnings. However demand may not be at constant levels. Some work may be seasonal or subject to the health of the economy.

Before taking the plunge and going self employed do some planning, which is were I went wrong. May be you do something as a hobby that earns a bit of pocket money. That is a whole kettle of fish different from doing something as your main source of income. If that is not going to pay the rent, or cover mortgage payments then either don't do it, or arrange part time work to make sure you have enough money.

Also if you can afford it get yourself an accountant as you will be amazed at what the tax office will cover as business expenses. For instance, get yourself a new laptop for work needs, as is the new television for the kitchen, and may be the games console for the kids ( I am a big kid despite being in my 50s). You can do your own online tax returns but these change every year and what a competent accountant could save you would cover their fees and then some.

Some aspects of being self employed I found useful like working from home and not having to commute for a few hours a week to an office or a warehouse. There is no boss to tell you what to do, and no colleagues to argue with. On the other hand periods of little work and working long hours for a few quid may mean having to rejoin the rat race. Working as a freelance writer didn't pay the bills, but as an aside I believe that at one point around 2017 I had written around 25% of the online reviews for online only florists in the Uk. I think I came up with enough made up names to write a 500 page novel or two.

If you can support yourself while getting your own business up and running then being self employed could be for you. You can be your own boss and do not have to work for others. Some people really enjoy the freedom of working for themselves and nobody else. They may never go back to being an employee. If they can make self employment financially viable then there may be no reason to ever start working for anybody else ever again.

## Chapter 22 - sometimes it's just one of them fecking days

Some days people that are generally happy in their vocation and satisfied with the team they are in have such an off day that they wonder why they bothered to turn up for work.

Bad days at the office, shop or warehouse can upgrade themselves into disastrously awful shifts. You know the kind of day within 30 minutes of getting out of your bed it occurs to you that turning the alarm clock off and not getting up would have been a far more sensible option. May be you spilt half of your coffee down your shirt at breakfast, or the shuttle bus knocked and you had to pay for a taxi to work. Perhaps your car broke down, cost a silly amount of cash to get fixed as well as losing a couple hours pay.

Then there can be times when whole teams, sections, departments or even workplaces can have a sh*t day. That could be a result of computer systems crashing, power cuts, flood or fire damage, or even being let down by another firm failing to do what it is supposed to do.

Office workers will dread a day that starts with the lifts breaking down, before all the photocopiers except for the slow one on the third floor stop working. Which would not have been so bad if had not been your office's turn to host the regional managers meeting and the CEO is the guest of honour and 20 flashily packs had supposed been finished two days ago…

May be it's Boxing Day and for all staff in a busy department store have to cope with the tills breaking down meaning the customers got annoyed and start arguing with them. In this scenario the colleagues that took the sensible option of taking the day off are considered the fortunate ones. To make matters worse it's 1990 and there is no such thing as online shopping yet...

Or just before you leave the house you break the button off your trousers but it does not matter as you have had your belt for five years and it seems good for another five. Except when you bend over to tie up your boot laces two minutes before clocking off time, and that same belt breaks in half. It is a good job yours truly was a boy scout and quickly turned a boot lace into an emergency belt!

# Chapter 23 – the fine art of tossing it off

No matter what a person's position within a company some days or nights there is simply nothing better than tossing it off, doing feck all, even if it's just for a few minutes. Those minutes of doing absolutely nothing, can be sheer bliss!

Depending on your position and role within a company the chances of being able to successfully toss it off can vary greatly. The busier a role normally is the harder it can be to get away with doing nothing, even for just a few minutes. On the other hand if you are fortunate enough to have a quieter role, or one with peaks and troughs the better the prospects are for tossing it off. Ten minutes here for a quick brew, another 20 minutes for going to the toilet (or checking your texts or playing a game on your phone).

Three tips about tossing it off:

1) make sure that your supervisors or managers believe that you are doing something else, preferably working.

2) ensure that wherever you are tossing it off gives you a full view of supervisors and managers allowing you to see them approaching so you can get back into position and they have no idea what you were doing.

3) supervisors or managers that are tossing it off can decide whether to include their staff in extra breaks or they can have such breaks on the sly .

Tossing it off when you are a sole trader is no where near as much fun as it is when you are a worker, supervisor, or manager. It's also a pointless exercise as you have still got to do the work, and you are the only one that can do it anyway.

# Chapter 24 - Robots, why have to deal with people?

Since the 1970s some companies have tried to replace people with robots to boost efficiency and productivity.

Here are the pros of doing so:

Robots do not to drink, eat or go to the toilet

They do not complain

Robots can't talk behind the managers' back or ignore supervisors

They can't go on strike

Robots do not need pay rises

The cons of robots :

People are still needed to install and repair robots

Robots can't make mistakes but the people who build, programme and repair them can

They will eventually become obsolete or need to be replaced if repairs are no longer possible

## Have you seen the Terminator films?

# Glossary

## Words and phrases to be embraced by the cynical and avoided like the plague by management or the ambitious

Alienation / alienated - use of this word should be regarded as a danger sign by management as it demonstrates members of staff are p•seed off with how things are. Particularly bad if used by trade union shop stewards

Ar•e licker / brown noser - somebody who bends over backwards to get approval from other people higher up the managerial ladder than themselves. They may do extra tasks or make overly nice comments to gain promotion, rewards or better treatment than their colleagues. Cynics and those who do not get on well with management are better off keeping away from ar•e lickers.

Business needs - an excuse that managers and supervisors use when they do not want to do anything for their staff, such as allowing day offs due to domestic emergencies or health appointments etc.

Common sense - the use of this phrase demonstrates that the user has considered the latest proposal(s) from management and knows it is / they are sh•te. Not to be confused with the exceedingly dull book by Thomas Paine.

Communication - if staff, supervisors or lower management use this word then it demonstrates there isn't any or if there is that it isn't working.

Daft - a little less cynical than using common sense but the uttering of this word indicates that the decision or process being discussed is not approved of.

Dedicated - someone that is committed to doing their job efficiently and may often go the extra mile to do so. Without having people doing extra roles many companies would achieve less. Bosses and cynics alike may refer to those who are highly committed as mugs or fools, but for different reasons.

Efficiency - from the management point of view getting one worker to do the work of at least 3 workers. In contrast from the worker perspective it is getting the most amount of work done for the least amount of effort and the maximum level of pay for doing so.

Goodwill - a factor that might not be easy to measure yet if staff have it then it needs to be nurtured instead of frittered away. It is the willingness to do things that benefit the team as a whole though it might gain individuals rewards they will extra things to help out.

Gross misconduct - when a member of staff or management have done something so bad that they get fired instantly.

Head office / Headquarters - in larger companies or organisations the place where the main decisions are made that can be put into place throughout the whole firm for better or worse. Sometimes these get it spot on, and at other times cause absolute bedlam.

Idiotic - usually relates to any decisions made by senior management or headquarters either without consulting, or ignoring the advice of lesser managers, supervisors and workers.

Incentive - the bullish•t managers come up with to tempt workers to work harder. Sometimes they might even keep their promises, but don't count on it.

Information - something that could be really useful if management ever used it, or took notice of what their staff told them about.

I was only doing as I was told - a slightly less sinister variation of I was just obeying orders (A KA the Nuremberg Defence) used by anybody that blindly follows managerial orders even if these are dangerous, idiotic or downright immoral.

LFS - lazy fecker syndrome, somebody who wants to do absolutely nothing all day every day, can be unemployed or just turns up to work, does feck all and gets paid for it.

Logic - prolific use of this word could get the person using it into serious bother, it is almost P45 behaviour. Never use it in the same sentence as common sense. Use of the L word states that whoever is using it thinks that management have lost the plot big time (if they ever had it in the first place).

Listen - a highly important aspect of communication and good workforce relations that too many managers, some supervisors and workers fail to do. Plenty of arguments and disputes could be averted or less serious if everyone took notice of all that was said.

Manager - the boss, the gaffer or the person in charge of a workplace, or a department or team within it. The one who can manage things in a good way, or be a wreaking ball either inadvertently or by design.

Manners - simply being polite to one another. If all team members are polite then it helps to build mutual respect. Managers and supervisors that ask workers to do things politely and thank them are far more likely to earn good will.

Minister - for those who work in the public sector / civil service changes in public policies can bring about big changes in the ways they do their jobs, and do doubt these could be reversed at any given moment (humming the song "The Minister" by The Move as I type).

NAFA - Not Another Fecking Acronym , an acronym I learned in my civil service days. Used to show how annoying too many acronyms or the over use of jargon can be at work.

PITFA - Pain in the fecking ar*e, somebody who is simply annoying beyond words. Can describe any boss, colleague, customer, or supervisor that makes life unbearable for others they come into contact with, especially you.

Targets - one of the most common methods of measuring the productivity or effectiveness of management, supervisors and workers. Basically staff are expected to complete a certain number of tasks per hour or within each shift. When these are set to an achievable and realistic levels then they be an incentive. However when the expected quota is too high then it can be a disincentive. Unrealistic numbers often leads to an unhealthy fixation with meeting the quota at the expense of quality, cutting corners or falsified data.

Team - the basis of many companies and organisations are groups of people or teams. Depending on the size of companies there may be a small number of teams or many groups. Each one could have a handful of members or hundreds. The trick is to get each member as part of the whole, and if that is achieved make sure it is maintained.

Why? - If there is a simple word that can have bosses regard someone as a troublemaker instantly this is probably the one. Simply by asking this one word question a person is showing that they doubt the rationale of what they have been told even if they accept the authority of the person telling them. It is a question that should be easy to answer, yet if bosses do not know the reason something is being done the way it is, or they disagree with what is happening, then it can be really difficult to answer.

Work to rule - a phrase used by unions to indicate that they and their members are not seeing eye to eye with management and will only carry out the roles in their job description. It is a sign that bosses have lost the goodwill of their staff. Sometimes if working to rule does not alter management behaviour it can be the prelude to strikes.

Finally, no task is so important that you can't make a brew and let it go cold.

PS what the gaffer doesn't know wont hurt them. But a proactive gaffer will know your getting a drink and will ask for one themselves.

PPS – If you want blood you can't fecking have mine!

Printed in Great Britain
by Amazon